DIA
DS.

70   65

KINGSTON, JAMAICA, FROM THE COMMERCIAL ROOMS

N O R T H   A T L A N T I C

O C E A N

N D S

Bahama or Lucayo

L. or Turk Is
Turk Is

Abreojos or
Square Handkerchief
Bank

Bajo de Plata
or Silver R.

Bank

Bajo Navidad

Vega France

Scott's B.

Puerto Franco

Samana Pt. & c.

Port Jackson

VIRGIN Is
Anegada
Horse Shoe

Pt. Engano

M. Ienguila
Desecho
Aguada
Arecivo

Virgin Gorda

Tortola
Van Dyke

Pt. Braquen
Pt. Espada
Francois
Anasco
Mayaguez
Mona
P.to Morillo

PORTO RICO
S.t German

C. S. Juan
Virgin Passage
S.t Thomas
S.t John
Danger I.
Anguilla

St. Martin

St. Bartholomeo

Sabana
S.t Saltalona
S.ta Saona

Maja
P.to Guanica

Vieque

S.ta Cruz
Boca del Infierno

Bird Ls

p.ta Cruz
Fredericksted

Guava del Maceos

S.t Cruz

Saba
S.t Eustatius

Palmetto Pt.

Great Pt. & Har.

Barbuda
Spanish Pt.

St. Christopher
Basse Terre
Charlestown
Nevis
Redonda

S.t John
Falmouth & English Har.

Antigua

Montserrat

Plymouth

Port
Louis
Gr. Morne
Basse terre

A Terre & Pt. Louis

Guadaloupe

Ann Deseada
Castle Pt.

Mariegalante

C A R I B B E E

L E E W A R D

20

The Map Drawn & Engraved by J. Rapkin.

Marlin!

BIG FISH

BOOKS

LIMITED EDITION

1992

Marlin!

Ernest Hemingway

PHOTOGRAPHS BY
ROBERTO HERRERA SOTOLONGO

K

Hemingway in Cuba

Gabriel García Márquez

RNEST

MILLER HEMINGWAY arrived in Havana for the first time in April, 1928.

"Fishing," he wrote, "was what brought us to Cuba." It was not a case of love at first sight, but a slow, arduous process, whose intimacies appear scattered and in code throughout most of the work of his maturity. In 1932, on his second trip to Cuba to fish for marlin, he seemed convinced that he had at last found a stable home in Key West where his son had been born and where he had finished his second novel, and where no doubt he had planted a tree to become the complete man of the proverb. From that time on he made innumerable trips to and from Cuba, accompanied by his crony, Joe Russell, owner of Sloppy Joe's in Key West, who apparently used fishing as a screen behind which he carried on more productive occupations.

"He once carried from Cuba [to Key West]

the biggest cargo of liquor ever known," wrote Hemingway. Contraband liquor, of course, at a time when drunks in the United States agonized with thirst under Prohibition. But those equivocal excursions, which were anything but literary, allowed Hemingway to come in contact with the good people of the sea who were to become his friends until he died, and who revealed to him a world that was to enrich his future writing.

In [this] article, published in the July, 1949, issue of *Holiday*, Hemingway disclosed who were his Cuban friends at that time. "Lottery ticket sellers you have known for years, policemen you have given fish to and who have done favors in their turn, bumboatmen who lose their earnings standing shoulder to shoulder with you in the betting pit at a jai-alai fronton and friends passing in motorcars along the harbor and ocean boulevard who wave and you wave to but cannot recognize at that distance." In other words, even then Hemingway thought of himself as a familiar character in the streets of Havana.

In those days he became acquainted as well with the Floridita, a seafood bar-restaurant established in the previous century that exists today with the same golden frieze and the same episcopal drapes. There the daiquiri cocktail was created, a happy combination of the diaphanous rum of the island, crushed ice and lemon juice, which Hemingway helped to make known throughout half the world. But as he was to write later, his main interest in the place was not so much its food and drink, but his desire to meet the tempestuous current of his countrymen who passed through the city.

"There are people there from all the states and from places where you have lived," he wrote. "There are also Navy ships in, cruise ships, Customs and Immigration agents, gamblers, embassy characters, aspiring writers, firmly or poorly established writers, senators on the town, the physicians and surgeons who come for conventions, Lions, Elks, Moose, Shriners, American Legion members, Knights of Columbus, beauty contest winners, characters who have gotten into a little trouble and pass a note in by the doorman, characters who get killed next week, characters who will be killed next year... not to mention your Cuban friends."

When Hemingway reminisced that way he had already won the Nobel Prize. More than a journalistic remembrance, it reads like nostalgia's telephone directory. It is difficult to reread his work now without recognizing many of the characters from that list, changed in time and place and transformed by the printed word, but hopelessly marked by the baptismal sin of the Floridita, where there is today a bust of Hemingway in a niche in the wall, and where an old bartender from his time never tires of showing tourists the bar stool where he used to sit.

HEMINGWAY LIVED IN CUBA a total of 22 years. In [the] article published in 1949, he tried to answer the question about why he lived there such a long time, but he got lost in a maze of diverse and contradictory reasons.

He talked about the fresh, caressing morning breeze on warm days, he talked about being able to breed fighting cocks, of the lizards that lived in the grapevines, of the 18 different kinds of mangoes in his courtyard, of the Sports Club just down the road where one could bet big money at pigeon-shooting matches and he spoke once more of the Gulf Stream which was only 45 minutes from his house and where he found the best and most abundant fishing he had ever seen in his life.

In the midst of so many justifications,

rather elusive ones, he interpolated a revealing paragraph: "You live in Cuba because you can plug the bell in the party-line telephone with paper, so that you won't have to answer and that you work as well there in those cool early mornings, as you ever have worked anywhere in the world."

At the end of the paragraph, either as a diversion or coquetry, he adds: "But those are professional secrets." This comment was unnecessary, for as most everybody knows, the reason for the choice of the place where one writes is one of the insoluble mysteries of literary creation.

rather elusive ones, he interpolated a revealing paragraph: "You live in Cuba because you can plug the bell in the party-line telephone with paper, so that you won't have to answer and that you work as well there in those cool early mornings, as you ever have worked anywhere in the world."

At the end of the paragraph, either as a diversion or coquetry, he adds: "But those are professional secrets." This comment was unnecessary, for as most everybody knows, the reason for the choice of the place where one writes is one of the insoluble mysteries of literary creation.

The line rose slowly and steadily and then the surface of the ocean bulged ahead of the boat and the fish came out. He came out unendingly and water poured from his sides. He was bright in the sun and his head and back were dark purple and in the sun the stripes on his sides showed wide and a light lavender. His sword was as long as a baseball bat and tapered like a rapier and he rose his full length from the water and then re-entered it, smoothly, like a diver and the old man saw the great scythe-blade of his tail go under and the line commenced to race out.

—ERNEST HEMINGWAY

THE OLD MAN AND THE SEA

Marlin!

Marlin!

EOPLE ASK

Y O U why you live in Cuba and you say it is because you like it. It is too complicated to explain about the early morning in the hills above Havana where every morning is cool and fresh on the hottest day in summer. There is no need to tell them that one reason you live there is because you can raise your own fighting cocks, train them on the place, and fight them anywhere that you can match them and that this is all legal. Maybe they do not like cockfighting anyway.

You do not tell them about the strange and lovely birds that are on the farm the year around, nor about all the migratory birds that come through, nor that quail come in the early mornings to drink at the swimming pool, nor about the different types of lizards that live and hunt in the thatched arbor at the end of the pool, nor the eighteen different

Marlin!

kinds of mangoes that grow on the long slope up to the house. You do not try to explain about our ball team—hard ball, not softball—where, if you are over forty, you can have a boy run for you and still stay in the game, nor which are the boys in our town that are really the fastest on the base paths.

You do not tell them about the shooting club just down the road, where we used to shoot the big live-pigeon matches for the large money, with Winston Guest, Tommy Shevlin, Thorwald Sanchez and Pichon Aguilera, and where we used to shoot matches against the Brooklyn Dodgers when they had fine shots like Curt Davis, Billy

Herman, Augie Galan and Hugh Casey. Maybe they think live-pigeon shooting is wrong. Queen Victoria did and barred it in England. Maybe they are right. Maybe it is wrong. It certainly is a miserable spectator sport. But with strong, really fast birds it is still the best participant sport for betting I know; and where we live it is legal.

You could tell them that you live in Cuba because you only have to put shoes on when you come into town, and that you can plug the bell in the party-line telephone with paper so that you won't have to answer, and that you work as well there in those cool early mornings as you ever have worked anywhere in the world. But those are professional secrets.

There are many other things you do not tell them. But when they talk to you about salmon fishing and what it costs them to fish the Restigouche, then, if they have not talked too much about how much it costs, and have talked well, or lovingly, about the salmon fishing, you tell them the biggest reason you live in Cuba is the great, deep blue river, three quarters of a mile to a mile deep and sixty to eighty miles across, that you can reach in thirty minutes from the door of your farmhouse, riding through beautiful country to get to it, that has, when the river is right, the finest fishing I have ever known.

When the Gulf Stream is running well, it is a dark blue and there are whirlpools along the edges. We fish it in a forty-foot cabin cruiser with a flying bridge equipped with topside controls, oversize outriggers big enough to skip a ten-pound bait in summer, and we fish four rods.

SEAGOING LADY

SOMETIMES WE KEEP Pilar, the fishing boat, in Havana harbor, sometimes in Cojimar, a fishing village seven miles east of Havana, with a harbor that is safe in summer and imminently unsafe in winter when there are northers or nor'westers. Pilar was built to be a fishing machine that would be a good sea boat in the heaviest kind of weather, have a minimum cruising range of five hundred miles, and sleep seven people. She carries three hundred gallons of gasoline in her tanks and one hundred and fifty gallons of water. On a long trip she can carry another hundred gallons of gas in small drums in her forward cockpit and the same extra amount of water in demijohns. She carries, when loaded full, 2400 pounds of ice.

Wheeler Shipyard, of New York, built her hull and modified it to our specifications, and we have made various changes in her since. She is a really sturdy boat, sweet in any kind of sea, and she has a very low-cut stern with a large wooden roller to bring big fish over. The flying bridge is so sturdy and so reinforced below you can fight fish from the top of the house.

Ordinarily, fishing out of Havana, we get a line out with a Japanese feather squid and a strip of pork rind on the hook, while we are still running out of the harbor. This is for tarpon, which feed around the fishing smacks anchored along the Morro Castle-Cabañas side of the channel, and for kingfish, which are often in the mouth of the main ship channel and over the bar, where the bottom fishermen catch snappers just outside the Morro.

This bait is fished on a twelve-foot No. 10 piano-wire leader from a 6/0 reel, full of fifteen-thread line and from a nine-ounce Tycoon tip. The biggest tarpon I ever caught with this rig weighed

135 pounds. We have hooked some that were much bigger but lost them to outgoing or incoming ships, to port launches, to bumboats, and to the anchor chains of the fishing smacks. You can plead with or threaten launches and bumboats when you have a big fish on and they are headed so that they will cut him off. But there is nothing you can do when a big tanker, or a cargo ship, or a liner is coming down the channel. So we usually put out this line when we can see the channel is clear and nothing is coming out; or after seven o'clock in the evening when ships will usually not be entering the harbor due to the extra port charges made after that hour.

Marlin!

      Coming out of the harbor I will be on the flying bridge steering and watching the traffic and the line that is fishing the feather astern. As you go out, seeing friends along the water front—lottery-ticket sellers you have known for years, policemen you have given fish to and who have done favors in their turn, bumboatmen who lose their earnings standing shoulder to shoulder with you in the bet-ting pit at the jai-alai fronton, and friends passing in motorcars along the harbor and ocean boulevard who wave and you wave to but cannot recognize at that distance, although they can see the Pilar and you on her flying bridge quite clearly—your feather jig is fishing all the time.

Behind the boulevards are the parks and buildings of old Havana and on the other side you are passing the steep slopes and walls of the fortress of Cabañas, the stone weathered pink and yellow, where most of your friends have been political prisoners at one time or another; and then you pass the rocky headland of the Morro, with O'Donnell, 1844, on the tall white light tower and then, two hundred yards beyond the Morro, when the stream is running well, is the great river.

WHERE THE
FLYING FISHES PLAY

SOMETIMES AS YOU leave the gray-green harbor water and Pilar's bows dip into the dark blue water a covey of flying fish will rise from under her bows and you will hear the slithering, silk-tearing noise they make when they leave the water.

If they are the usual size flying fish it does not mean so much as a sign, unless you see a man-of-war hawk working, dipping down after them if they go up again; but if they are the big three-pound, black-winged Bahian flyers that come out of the water as though they were shot out, and at the end of their soaring flight drop their tails to give the flight a new impulse and fly again and again, then it is a very good sign. Seeing the Bahian flyers is as sure a sign as any, except seeing fish themselves.

By now, Gregorio, the mate, has gotten the meat line out. The meat line is a new trick that I'll tell about later, because once it is out, and he wants to get it out fast to cover this patch of bottom before we get outside of the hundred-fathom curve, he must get outrigger baits out, since marlin

Marlin!

will come in over this bottom any time the stream is running and the water is blue and clear.

Gregorio Fuentes has been mate on Pilar since 1938. He is fifty years old this summer and went to sea in sail from Lanzarota, one of the smaller Canary Islands, when he was four. I met him at Dry Tortugas when he was captain of a fishing smack and we were both stormbound there in a very heavy northeast gale in 1928. We went on board his smack to get some onions. We wanted to buy the onions, but he gave them to us, and some rum as well, and I remember thinking he had the cleanest ship that I had ever seen. Now after ten years I know that he would rather keep a ship clean, and paint and varnish, than he would fish. But I know, too, that he would rather fish than eat or sleep.

We had a great mate before Gregorio, named Carlos Gutierrez, but someone hired him away from me when I was away at the Spanish Civil War. It was wonderful luck to find Gregorio, and his seamanship has saved Pilar in three hurricanes. So far, knocking on wood, we have never had to put in a claim on the all-risk marine insurance policy carried on her; and Gregorio was the only man to stay on board a small craft in the October,

1944, hurricane when it blew 180 mph true, and small craft and Navy vessels were blown up onto the harbor boulevard and up onto the small hills around the harbor. He also rode out the 1948 hurricane on her.

By now, as you have cleared the harbor, Gregorio has the meat line out and is getting the outrigger baits out and, it being a good day, you are getting flying fish up and pushing to the eastward into the breeze. The first marlin you see can show within ten minutes of leaving your moorings, and so close to the Morro that you can still see the curtains on the light.

MARLIN!

HE MAY COME behind the big, white wooden teaser that is zig-zagging and diving between the two inside lines. He may show behind an outrigger bait that is bouncing and jumping over the water. Or he may come racing from the side, slicing a wake through the dark water, as he comes for the feather.

When you see him from the flying bridge he will look first brown and then dark purple as he rises in the water, and his pectoral fins, spread wide as he comes to feed, will be a light lavender

Marlin!

color and look like widespread wings as he dives just under the surface. He will look, in the sea, more like a huge submarine bird than a fish.

Gregorio, if he sees him first will shout, "Feesh! Feesh, Papa, feesh!"

If you see him first you leave the wheel, or turn it over to Mary, your wife, and go to the stern end of the house and say "Feesh" as calmly as possible to Gregorio, who has always seen him by then, too, and you lean over and he hands you up the rod the marlin is coming for, or, if he is after the teaser, he hands you up the rod with the feather and pork rind on.

All right, he is after the teaser and you are racing-in the feather. Gregorio is keeping the teaser, a tapering, cylindrical piece of wood two feet long, with a curve cut in its head that makes it dive and dance when towed, away from the marlin. The marlin is rushing it and trying to grab it. His bill comes out of water as he drives toward it. But Gregorio keeps it just out of his reach. If he pulled it all the way in, the fish might go down. So he is playing him as a bullfighter might play a bull, keeping the lure just out of his range, and yet never denying it to him, while you race-in the feather.

Mary is saying, "Isn't he beautiful? Oh,

Marlin!

Papa, look at his stripes and that color and the color of his wings. Look at him! "

"I'm looking at him," you say, and you have the feather now abreast of the teaser, and Gregorio sees it and flicks the teaser clear, and the marlin sees the feather. The big thing that he chased, and that looked and acted like a crippled fish, is gone. But here is a squid, his favorite food, instead.

The marlin's bill comes clear out of water as he hits the feather and you see his open mouth and, as he hits it, you lower the rod that you have held as high as you could, so the feather goes out of sight into his mouth. You see it go in, and the mouth shuts and you see him turn, shining silver, his stripes showing as he turns.

As he turns his head you hit him, striking hard, hard and hard again, to set the hook. Then, if he starts to run instead of jumping, you hit him three or four times more to make sure, because he might just be holding feather, hook and all, tight in his jaws and running away with it, still unhooked. Then he feels the hook and jumps clear. He will jump straight up all clear of the water, shaking himself. He will jump straight and stiff as a beaked bar of silver. He will jump high and long, shedding

Marlin!

drops of water as he comes out, and making a splash like a shell hitting when he enters the water again. And he will jump, and jump, and jump, sometimes on one side of the boat, then crossing to the other so fast you see the belly of the line whipping through the water, fast as a racing ski turn.

Sometimes he will get the leader over his shoulder (the hump on his back behind his head) and go off greyhounding over the water, jumping continuously and with such an advantage in pull, with the line in that position, that you cannot stop him, and so Mary has to back Pilar fast and then turn, gunning both motors, to chase him.

You lose plenty of line making the turn to chase him. But he is jumping against the friction of the belly of the line in the water which keeps it taut, and when, reeling, you recover that belly and have the fish now broadside, then astern again, you have control of him once more. He will sound now and circle, and then you will gradually work him closer and closer and then in to where Gregorio can gaff him, club him and take him on board.

That is the way it should go ideally; he should sound, circle and you should work him gradually alongside or on either quarter of the stern, and then gaff him, club him and bring him on board. But it doesn't always go that way. Sometimes when he gets up to the boat he will start the whole thing all over again and head out for the northwest, jumping again as fresh, seemingly, as when he was first hooked, and you have to chase him again.

Sometimes, if he is a big striped marlin, you will get him within thirty feet of the boat and he will come no farther, swimming, with his wings spread, at whatever speed and direction you elect to move. If you don't move, he will be up and under the boat. If you move away from him, he will stay there, refusing to come in one inch, as strong a fish for his weight as any in the world and as stubborn.

(Bonefish angler, On your way! You never saw a bonefish in mile-deep water, nor up against the tackle striped marlin have to face sometimes. Nor did you know how your bonefish would act after he had jumped forty-three times clean out of water. Your bonefish is a smart fish, very conservative, very strong too. Too smart by far to jump, even if he could. I do not think he can, myself. And the only nonjumping fish that has a patent of nobility in our books is the wahoo. He *can* jump, too, if he wants to. He will do it sometimes when he takes the bait. Also, bonefish angler, your fish might be as fat and as short of wind, at four hundred pounds, as some of the overstuffed Nova Scotia tuna are. But do not shoot, bonefish angler; at four hundred pounds, your fish might be the strongest thing in the sea, the strongest fish that ever lived; so strong no one would ever want to hook into one. But tell me confidentially: would he jump? . . . Thank you very much. I thought not.)

This dissertation has not helped you any if you have a strong, male, striped marlin on and he decides he won't be lifted any closer. Of course you could loosen up the drag and work away from him and wear him out that way. But that is the way sharks get fish. We like to fight them close to the boat and take them while they are still strong. We will gaff an absolutely green fish, one that has not been tired at all, if by any fluke we can get him close enough.

Since 1931, when I learned that was how to keep fish from being hit by sharks, I have never lost a marlin nor a tuna to a shark, no matter how shark-infested the waters fished. We try to fight them fast, but never rough. The secret is for the angler never to rest. Any time he rests the fish is resting. That gives the fish a chance to get strong again, or to get down to a greater depth; and the odds lengthen that something may close in on him.

So now, say, you have this marlin down thirty feet, pulling as strong as a horse. All you have to do is stay with him. Play him just this side of breaking strain, but do it softly. Never jerk on him. Jerking will only hurt him or anger him. Either or both will make him pull harder. He is as strong as a horse. Treat him like a horse. Keep your maximum possible strain on him and you will convince him and bring him in. Then you gaff him, club him for kindness and for safety, and bring him on board.

You do not have to kill a horse to break

him. You have to convince him, and that is what you have to do with a truly strong, big fish after the first jumps, which correspond to a wild horse's bucking, are over. To do this, you have to be in good condition.

There is tackle made now, and there are fishing guides expert in ways of cheating with it, by which anybody who can walk up three flights of stairs, carrying a quart bottle of milk in each hand, can catch game fish over five hundred pounds without even having to sweat much.

There is old-fashioned tackle with which you can catch really big fish in a short time, thus ensuring they will not be attacked by sharks. But you have to be a fisherman or, at least, in very good shape to use it. But this is the tackle that will give you the greatest amount of sport with the smaller and medium-sized marlin. You don't need to be an athlete to use it. You ought to be in good condition. If you are not, two or three fish will put you in condition. Or they may make you decide marlin fishing in the Gulf Stream is not your sport.

In almost any other sport requiring strength and skill to play or practice, those practicing the sport expect to know how to play it, to have at least moderate ability and to be in some sort of condition. In big-game fishing they will come on board in ghastly shape, incapable of reeling in 500 yards of line, simply line, with no question of there being a fish on it, and yet full of confidence that they can catch a fish weighing twice or three times their weight.

They are confident because it has been done. But it was never done honestly, to my knowledge, by completely inexperienced and untrained anglers, without physical assistance from the guides, mates and boatmen, until the present winch reels, unbreakable rods and other techniques were invented which made it possible for any angler, no matter how incompetent, to catch big fish if he could hold and turn the handle of a winch.

The International Game Fish Association, under the auspices of the American Museum of Natural History, has tried to set a standard of sporting fishing and to recognize records of fish taken honestly and sportingly according to these standards. It has had considerable success in these and other fields. But as long as charter boats are extremely expensive, and both guides and their anglers want results above everything else, big-game fishing will be closer to total war against big fish than to sport. Of course, it could never be considered an equal contest unless the angler had a hook in his mouth, as well as the fish. But insistence on that might discourage the sporting fishermen entirely.

Education as to what makes a big fish legitimately caught has been slow, but it has progressed steadily. Very few guides or anglers shoot or harpoon hooked fish any more. Nor is the flying gaff much used .

The use of wire line, our meat line, is a deadly way of fishing, and no fish caught that way could possibly be entered as a sporting record. But we use it as a way of finding out at what depths

fish are when they are not on the surface. It is a
scientific experiment, the results are carefully
noted, and what it catches are classed in our books
as fish caught commercially. Its carefully recorded
results will surely provide valuable information for
the commercial fisherman, and its use is justified
for that end. It is also a very rough, tough, punishing
way to catch big fish and it puts the angler who
practices it, fishing standing up, not sitting in a
chair, into the condition he needs to be able to
fight fish honestly with the sporting tackle that
allows the fish to run, leap and sound to his fullest
ability and still be caught within an hour by the

angler, if the angler knows how to handle big fish.

Fighting a really big fish, fast and unaided, never resting, nor letting the fish rest, is comparable to a ten-round fight in the ring in its requirements for good physical condition. Two hours of the same, not resting, not letting the fish rest, is comparable to a twenty-round fight. Most honest and skillful anglers who lose big fish do so because the fish whips them, and they cannot hold him when he decides, toward the end of the fight, to sound and, sounding, dies.

Once the fish is dead, sharks will eat him if any are about. If he is not hit by sharks, bringing him up, dead, from a great depth is one of the most difficult phases of fishing for big fish in deep water.

We have tried to work out tackle which would give the maximum sport with the different fish, small, medium, large and oversize, at the different months of the year when they run. Since their runs overlap it has been necessary to try to have always a margin of safety in the quantity of line. In a section at the end of the article this tackle is described. It would not suit purists, or members of some light-tackle clubs; but remember we fish five months out of the year in water up to a mile deep, in a current that can make a very big sea with the trade wind blowing against it, and in waters that are occasionally infested with sharks. We could catch fish with the very lightest tackle, I believe. It would prove nothing, since others have done it, and we would break many fish off to die. Our ideal is to catch the fish with tackle that you can really pull on and which still permits the fish to jump and run as freely as possible.

Then, altogether apart from that ideal, there is the meat line. This is 800 yards of monel wire of eighty-five-pound test which, fished from an old Hardy six-inch reel and old Hardy No. 5 rod, will sink a feather jig down so that it can be trolled in thirty-five fathoms if you put enough wire out. When there are no fish on the surface at all, this goes down where they are. It catches everything: wahoo out of their season when no one has caught one on the surface for months; big grouper; huge dog snappers, red snappers, big kingfish; and it catches marlin when they are deep and not coming up at all. With it we eat, and fill the freezing unit, on days when you would not have caught a fish surface-trolling. The fight on the wire which actually tests no more than thirty-nine-thread line but is definitely wire, not line, is rugged muscle-straining, punishing, short and anything but sweet. It is in a class with steer bull-dogging, bronc riding and other ungentle sports. The largest marlin caught in 1948 on the meat line was a 210-pound striped fish. We caught him when we had fished three days on the surface and not seen a thing.

Now we are anxious to see what the meat line will dredge into during those days in August and September, when there are flat calms, and the huge fish are down deep and will not come up. When you hook a marlin on the wire he starts shaking his head, then he bangs it with his bill, then he sees if he can outpull you. Then if he can't, he finally comes up to see what is the matter. What we are anxious to find out is what happens if he ever gets the wire over his shoulder and starts to go. They can go, if they are big enough, wire and all. We plan to try to go with him. There is a chance we could make it, if Pilar makes the turn fast enough. That will be up to Mary.

The really huge fish always head out to the northwest when they make their first run. If you are ever flying across between Havana and Miami, and looking down on the blue sea, and you see something making splashes such as a horse dropped off a cliff might make, and behind these splashes a black boat with green topside and decks is chasing, leaving a white wake behind her—that will be us.

If the splashes look sizable from the height that you are flying, and they are going out to the northwest, then wish us plenty of luck. Because we will need it.

In the meantime, what we always hope for is fish feeding on the surface, up after the big flying fish, and that whoever is a guest on the boat, unless he or she has fished before, will hook something under one hundred and fifty pounds to start with. Any marlin from thirty pounds up, on proper tackle, will give a new fisherman all the excitement and all the exercise he can assimilate, and off the marlin grounds along the north Cuban coast he might raise twenty to thirty in a day, when they are running well. The most I ever caught in one day was seven. But Pepe Gomez-Mena and Martin Menocal caught twelve together in one day, and I would hate to bet that record would not be beaten by them, or by some of the fine resident and visiting sportsmen who love and know the marlin fishing of the great river that moves along Cuba's northern coast.

ERNEST HEMINGWAY'S
TACKLE SPECIFICATIONS

WHITE MARLIN RUN

April—May—Early June.

Gear for the feather jig, fished astern, with pork-rind strip on the hook: Rod, 9 oz. or 12 oz. tip; *Reel,* 6/0; 500 yards #15 thread line; 12-foot piano-wire leader #9 or #10; 8/0 or 9/0 O'Shaughnessy hook, or 8/0 Mustad, smallest type of Japanese feather jig (white) and three-inch strip of pork rind attached. (This gives a beautiful motion in the water. Of white marlin hooked we average six out of ten on the feather compared to the baits.)

First rod (light for smaller bait) of the two out-rigger rods: Rod, 14 oz. tip; *Reel,* 9/0; 600 yards of #18 thread line; 14-foot piano-wire leader #10 or #11; 10/0 Mustad hook.

Baits: small mullet, strip bait, boned needle fish, small cero mackerel, small or medium size fly-ing fish, fresh squid and cut baits.

Second rod of two outriggers: 14 oz. tip; *Reel,* 9/0; 400 yards of #18 thread line, spliced to 150 yards of #21 thread, on the outside for when the fish is close to the boat. 14-foot piano-wire leader #11; 11/0 or 12/0 Mustad hook.

Baits: big cero mackerel, medium and large mullet, large strip baits, flying fish and good-sized squid.

Above rod is designed to attract any big fish that might be mixed in with the smaller run.

Marlin!

BIG MARLIN RUN

July—August—September—October.

(Fish from 250 to over 1000 pounds.)

Feather is fished same as ever, since after white marlin are gone it will catch school tuna, albacore, bonito and dolphin. An extra rod is in readiness, equipped with feather jig in case schools of above fish are encountered.

Outrigger rods: Either 22 or 24 oz. tips. (The best I have found, outside of the old Hardy Hickory-Palakona bamboo #5, are those made by Frank O'Brien of Tycoon Tackle, Inc. His rods are incomparably the best I know made today.)

Reels: 12/0 or 14/0 Hurdy, and two 14/0 Finor for guests. If inexperienced anglers want to catch big fish they need the advantage the Finor changeable gear ratio reel gives them.

Line: all the reels will hold without jamming of either 36 or 39 thread good Ashaway linen line. We use this line for years, testing it, discarding any rotted by the sun, and splicing on more as needed. Leaders are 14 1/2 foot stainless-steel cable.

Hooks: 14/0 Mustad, bent in the crook of the shank to give the point an offset hooking drive.

Baits: Albacore and bonito, whole, up to

seven pounds and barracuda, whole, up to five and six pounds. These are the best. Alternative baits are large cero mackerel, squid, big mullet and yellow jacks, runners and big needlefish. Of all baits, the whole bonito and albacore have proved, with us, the best for attracting really big marlin.

Ernest Miller Hemingway, the grandpa of terse dialogue, gripping understatement and swashbuckling story plots, is widely considered the most innovative American writer of the 20th century. As a cub reporter for the *Kansas City Star*, Hemingway honed the reporting skills that formed his rugged, stark style. The author, much like the sensitive-yet-tough heroes that peopled his books, spent his life roving the world, from Spanish bullrings and Parisian cafes to the fishing villages of Key West and Havana. (Don't most exotic locations sport an Ernest Hemingway Bar?) These travels were the grist for his best books: *The Sun Also Rises*, *To Have and Have Not* and *A Moveable Feast*. *The Old Man and the Sea*, drawn from the fishing trips in *Marlin!*, won a Pulitzer in 1952. Two years later, Hemingway was awarded the Nobel Prize for Literature. He committed suicide in Sun Valley, Idaho, in 1961.

Books by Ernest Hemingway

THREE STORIES AND TEN POEMS (1923)

THE TORRENTS OF SPRING (1926)

THE SUN ALSO RISES (1926)

MEN WITHOUT WOMEN (1928)

IN OUR TIME (1930)

WINNER TAKE NOTHING (1932)

A FAREWELL TO ARMS (1932)

DEATH IN THE AFTERNOON (1932)

THE GREEN HILLS OF AFRICA (1935)

TO HAVE AND HAVE NOT (1937)

THE FIFTH COLUMN (1938)

FOR WHOM THE BELL TOLLS (1938)

THE FIRST FORTY-NINE HOURS (1938)

ACROSS THE RIVER AND INTO THE TREES (1950)

THE OLD MAN AND THE SEA (1952)

Posthumous

A MOVEABLE FEAST (1964)

ISLANDS IN THE STREAM (1970)

THE NICK ADAMS STORIES (1972)

HEMINGWAY'S SELECTED LETTERS (1981)

THE DANGEROUS SUMMER (1985)

THE GARDEN OF EDEN (1986)

A NOTE ON THE TYPE

Marlin!'s text face is Californian, designed by type wizard
Frederic Goudy in 1936, expressly for the University of
California. He called the italic version of this font his best
design. Goudy disciple Roger Black and the Font Bureau have
painstakingly re-created the entire Californian family for the
Macintosh. The Big Fish logotype is a scuffed-up version of
Saks Goudy Bold, designed for Saks Fifth Avenue by Goudy in
1934. *Marlin!* was designed by John Miller and composed on a
Macintosh IIcx.

A NOTE ON THE LEAPING FISH

All marlin and the Big Fish logo were created by Neil Shigley.

SPECIAL THANKS TO

Eduardo Datangel, Roger Black, Tom Morgan, John Martin,
Nick Lyons, Annie Barrows, Tom Jenks, Pat Tompkins, Marie
Marino, Neil Shigley, Scott Walker, Peter Howard, Copyright
Studio/Paris, Pinnacle Publishing Services. West Indies map
courtesy of Lyons Ltd., San Francisco.

Marlin! was printed at Anchor & Acorn Press (jacket) and
Haddon Craftsmen (interior). All production and printing was
superbly coordinated by Litho & Graphics, San Francisco.

SPECIAL THANKS TO

Eduardo Datangel, Roger Black, Tom Morgan, John Martin,
Nick Lyons, Annie Barrows, Tom Jenks, Pat Tompkins, Marie
Marino, Neil Shigley, Scott Walker, Peter Howard, Copyright
Studio/Paris, Pinnacle Publishing Services. West Indies map
courtesy of Lyons Ltd., San Francisco.

Marlin! was printed at Anchor & Acorn Press (jacket) and
Haddon Craftsmen (interior). All production and printing was
superbly coordinated by Litho & Graphics, San Francisco.

BIG FISH
BOOKS

BIG FISH BOOKS are published in San Francisco
by John Miller. In addition to limited editions, Big Fish
does book design, editing and packaging.

THE MAYBECK BUILDING : 1736 STOCKTON No 4
SAN FRANCISCO, CALIFORNIA 94133 415.986.5030

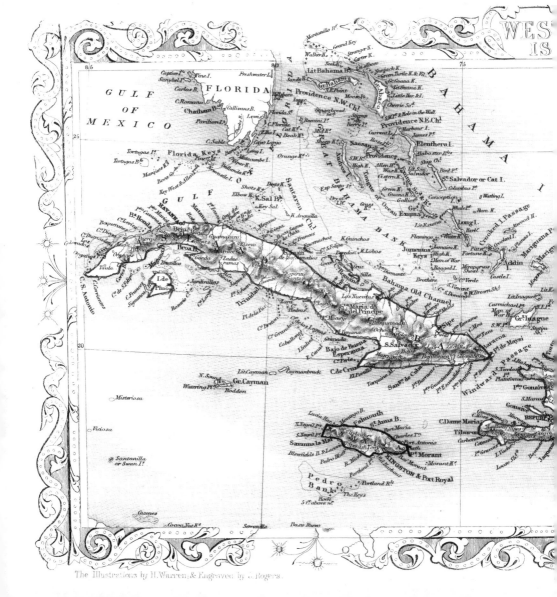

GULF
OF
MEXICO

FLORIDA

Providence N.W.Ch¹
Providence N.E.Ch¹
Nassau
Eleuthera I.
Providence
S¹ Salvador or Cat I.

BAHAMA

Florida Keys

GULF

GREAT BAHAMA BANK

Long I.
Crooked I. Passage
Gr.
Exuma
Flamingo
Lit.Exuma

Bahama Old Channel

Gr. Inague

HAVANNA

I. de
Pinos

Trinidad

S¹ª Maria de
del Principe

S. Salvador

Windward³
Passage

C. S¹ Antonio

Mysteriosa

Gr. Cayman
Boddon

Raymanbank

Pedro Ph

Lit. Cayman
Wattering Pt.

Vieiosa

Santanilla
or Swan Is¹

Savanna la Mar
Blewfields B.

Falmouth
S¹ Anns B.
Port Maria
Charles T¹
Port Antonio

C.Dame Maria
Tiburon

Carbonet

KINGSTON & Port Royal
S¹ Morant

Pedro
Banks

Portland Rh
The Revs
5 ft above w¹

Cazones
Cocoa Nut R³
Serranilla
Baxo Nuevo

The Illustrations by H. Warren, & Engraved by J. Rogers.